Teache s
for Guide g

THE ENORMOUS TURNIP

Teacher's notes by Alison Kelly
Roehampton University
and Suzanne Maile
Sheen Mount School

Contents

Essential information

National Curriculum level: 1A

Genre: adapted children's classic/traditional tale

Word count: 366

High frequency words

a	about	again	all	and	as	at
bed	big	but	called	cat	could	dog
for	go	help	he	his	just	last
more	next	night	off	once	one	out
over	pull	saw	some	that	the	then
they	this	three	time	two	up	very
went	with					

Interest words

enormous	turnip	puffing	panting	red in the face

Background
This traditional Russian tale has a cumulative structure, which both adds to the comic effect and helps children gain confidence by reading familiar patterns. The lively illustrations are full of humour (look out for the dancing animals) and, combined with the thought and speech bubbles, add imaginative additional narrative touches.

There is a double-page spread introducing the characters before the story begins, and a brief biography of Tolstoy, the original author, at the back of the book.

Introducing the story

Before you start the reading session or sessions, spend a little time preparing with your group.

If you can, start by producing a turnip. Ask the children if they know what it is. Can they guess what story they are going to read? (Some children may be familiar with the story in another version.) Note that it is unusual to find turnips for sale with the leaves intact so it might be helpful to show them where the leaves would have been.

If they haven't guessed it, say that they are going to read a story about a turnip. But no ordinary turnip...

Share learning objectives with your group.

The children are going to learn or practise the following:

- identifying and describing characters
- discussing the use of speech bubbles
- considering characters' moods
- predicting a storyline.

You might say:

- We are going to find out about the people in the story, what they are like and how they are feeling.
- We are going to look at the things they say.
- We are going to think about what happens next in the story.

Show the children a copy of the book.

Look at the front cover. Ask questions such as:

- What is the title of the book?
- What kind of book is it – fiction or non-fiction? What's the difference? How can we check?
- What does "enormous" mean? How big is enormous? Can we find the word that says "enormous"?

Give a brief introduction to the book. For example:

This book is all about a farmer who grew such a big turnip that he couldn't dig it up... Let's see what happens.

Now go on to the Walkthrough (see overleaf).

Walkthrough

The walkthrough allows you to "warm" the text for the children by taking them through it without actually reading it.

- You might use it to identify key vocabulary, language patterns and concepts that children could need support with
- You can identify phoneme-grapheme relationships that are to be practised
- It can be a way to identify key 'thinking points' in the story (e.g. where predictions might be made, characters' thoughts inferred and so on).

Using a copy of the book, look through it with the children. We have suggested pause points and prompts.

Pages 2-3 introduce the main characters.

You might say:

- Let's meet the characters in this book. Can you find: the farmer, his wife and so on?
- Can you see the leaves on the turnip?

Go on to pages 4-5.

You might say:

- Are all the characters on this page? Who are they?
- How are they feeling as the story begins?
- What are they all doing?
- Can you find the word that says "turnip"?

Go on to pages 8-9.

You might say:

- Look at the picture. What is the farmer doing? Take suggestions for his action and ask if they can read "tugged". If they don't know it, help them to blend the phonemes together: t/u/gg/ed.

Go on to pages 12-13.

You might say:

- What is happening here? What are they trying to do?
- Note the use of a speech bubble.
  Should we use a special voice to read the words in the bubble?
  Read the bubble together. Predict what might happen next.
- Look at "hugged".
  Can you read this word?
  (If necessary, make the link with "tugged" on page 8.)

Go on to pages 14-15.

You might say:

- Jack's parents are trying very, very hard. They are puffing and panting. Can you find the words that say "puffing and panting"? What do you think they mean?

Go on to pages 36-37.

You might say:

- Can you find the word "enormous"? Why has it been written in such a big font size?

The children should now be ready to read independently. This can be done over several sessions, depending on their experience and ability. We have allowed for two sessions, but you might take more or fewer.

Independent reading and strategy check

Before the children begin reading, include a strategy check to help them tackle difficult or unfamiliar words. **You might say:**

- Let's remember what we do when we can't read a word.

  Elicit suggestions from the children, e.g. blend the phonemes, read ahead.

Ask the children to read aloud, a little at a time, either all together or in turns, whilst you listen and monitor. Encourage them to use cues to work out unfamiliar words, and praise fluent reading or good use of strategies.

For assessment purposes, you may want to use the chart on pages 30–31 to note strategies that each child uses, or errors or comments that he or she makes, during the reading.

Now ask the children to read pages 2-25, whilst you monitor and record strategies.

This story has

a farmer,

his wife,

their son Jack,

2

a dog,

a cat,

a bird and

an **enormous** turnip.

One morning, the farmer went to his field. He wanted a turnip.

He saw one turnip with very big green leaves.

"I'll pick this one," thought the farmer.

6

The farmer tugged and tugged at the turnip.

The turnip didn't move.

9

The farmer's wife saw the farmer puffing and panting.

"I'll help," she called.

She hugged the farmer.

He grabbed the turnip leaves.

They both tugged and tugged.

But the turnip didn't move.

13

Pause after page 13.

You might say:

- The farmer's wife was very busy watering her flowers. Do you think she wanted to help her husband? What do you think her thought bubble might say?
- Do you think they will be able to pull the turnip up together?
- Who do you think might help next?

Now ask the children to read pages 14 - 25.

Jack held his mother's skirt.

She hugged the farmer.

The farmer grabbed the turnip leaves.

And they tugged and tugged until they were red in the face. But the turnip didn't move.

"Woof!" barked the farmer's dog. He raced into the field.

"Let's try again," said the farmer.

The dog pulled Jack's shirt.

20

Jack held his mother's skirt.

She hugged the farmer. The farmer grabbed the turnip leaves.

21

They all tugged and tugged as hard as they could.

But the turnip didn't move.

22

No one saw the cat arrive.

She bit the dog's tail.

23

The dog ripped Jack's shirt.

Jack tore his mother's skirt.

She let go of the farmer.

Pause after page 25.

You might say:

- How are all the characters feeling now?
- What about the cat? She looks very pleased with herself. Why?

Suggested session 2

If you are reading the story in two sessions, you might like to go over the story so far. What do the children remember from the previous session? Look through the first part of the book to refresh their memories.

When you are ready, ask the children to read pages 26-45, whilst you monitor and record strategies.

The farmer brushed the dirt off his clothes. "Let's try once more," he said.

Just then, a bird flew past.

"One, two, three... pull!" said the farmer.

The cat bit the dog's tail.

The bird pecked the cat's tail.

30

The dog pulled Jack's shirt.

31

Jack held his
mother's skirt.

The farmer grabbed the
turnip and everybody
tugged.

She hugged
the farmer.

32

They tugged and tugged
and tugged some more.

33

Slowly,

slowly,

very, very

slowly,

the turnip began to move.

"It's big,"
said the farmer.

"It's huge,"
said his wife.

35

"It's **enormous!**" cried Jack.

At last, the turnip popped out of the ground.

Pause after page 39.

You might say:

- They've got the turnip up – but it's not the end of the story. What do you think will happen next?

Now ask the children to read pages 40–45.

The farmer was very happy. "Time for bed," he said, yawning.

That night, he fell asleep with a smile on his face.

40

In the morning, Jack helped his mother chop up the turnip.

They ate turnip soup for lunch...

turnip soup for supper...

43

and turnip soup for breakfast...

every day for a month.

44

"Next year I'm growing carrots," said the farmer.

45

Pause after page 45.

You could ask:

- Why is the farmer going to grow carrots next year?
- Can you make up thought bubbles for Jack and the dog?

Now return to the text (see overleaf) to discuss whether the children's answers and predictions were correct, and talk about their approaches.

Return to the text

The return to the text allows you to reinforce teaching points, e.g. checking children's understanding, identifying and reinforcing successful decoding strategies.

Look through the story again to recap on strategies the children have used for decoding unfamiliar words (e.g. phonic, graphic, context or syntax).

You might say:

- I really liked the way (***child's name***) worked out how to read (***word or phrase***) – can you tell us how you did it?

Talk about the story as a whole.

You might ask:

- Were there any parts of the story that surprised you?
- Which part (or character or picture) did you like best?
- Did you like the ending? Can you think of a different way the story could have ended?
- Do you know any other stories like this?

You might also like to read and discuss the short "About the author" section at the end of the book. Do the children know anything about Russia, or any other Russian stories?

Further reading

First Reading Level Three

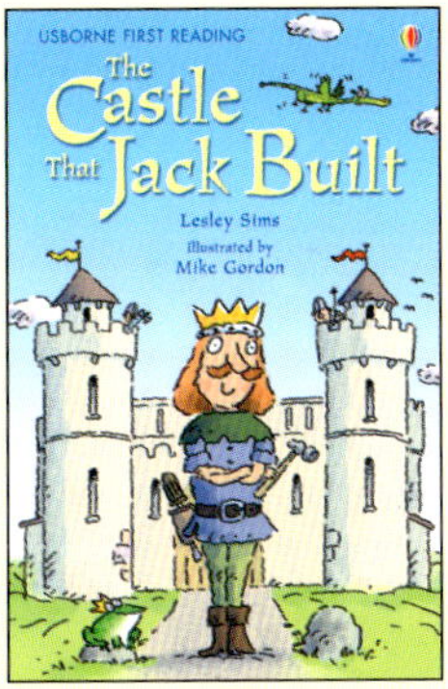

First Reading Level Four

There are over 30 titles available in the First Reading series, and more are being added all the time. To find out about all the titles available, go to **www.usborne.com**

Guided Reading Record

Text: *The Enormous Turnip – level 1 working towards level 2*

Class:...

Group:...

Date:...

Teacher/
Teaching Assistant:..

At Level 1A, it is expected that children:

1. Select books for personal reading and give reasons for choices.
2. Can distinguish between fiction and non-fiction texts and the different purposes for reading them.
3. Use syntax and context when reading for meaning.
4. Apply phonic knowledge and skills as the prime approach to reading.
5. Recognize the main events that shape different texts.
6. Read more challenging texts which can be decoded using acquired phonic knowledge and skills.
7. Read high frequency words automatically.

Name: *Comments:* *Target:*	*Name:* *Comments:* *Target:*
Name: *Comments:* *Target:*	*Name:* *Comments:* *Target:*
Name: *Comments:* *Target:*	*Name:* *Comments:* *Target:*

About the Usborne Reading Programme

The Usborne Reading Programme is a collection of over 150 titles for beginner readers, graded in seven levels from very beginners to fully confident readers. Launched in 2002, it has since sold almost 5 million copies worldwide.

The Usborne Reading Programme combines vivid, engaging writing with captivating full-colour illustration on every page. From classic tales to lively non-fiction, there is something to appeal to everyone.

From one level to the next, there is a clear progression in terms of subject, style, narrative length, sentence structure and vocabulary, giving children the satisfaction of mastering real books and making measurable progress without overstretching them and causing them to lose enthusiasm.

Non-fiction titles at all levels draw on the expertise of a range of specialists in their subject, ensuring that the books are not only engaging but authoritative: for example, Eva Schloss, stepsister of Anne Frank, advised on **Anne Frank**, and John Woolley of the Captain Cook Memorial Museum in Whitby advised on **Captain Cook**.

The Reading Programme advisers

The Reading Programme has been developed in consultation with **Alison Kelly**, a leading expert in the teaching of reading, who helped to draw up the seven-level framework (see pages 36-37). Alison worked for many years as a primary school teacher in London, and is currently a Senior Lecturer in Education at Roehampton University, teaching about all aspects of literacy.

Suzanne Maile is assistant headteacher at Sheen Mount Primary School in south-west London, a thriving school with a reputation for outstanding teaching and learning. Suzanne is responsible for curriculum development and initial teacher training at Sheen Mount, and has extensive experience in teaching guided reading at all levels. She is also a teacher tutor at Roehampton University, and a consultant teacher for Richmond LEA.

Together, Suzanne and Alison have chosen a selection of titles from the Reading Programme that are particularly suitable for guided reading, and produced comprehensive teacher's notes, packed with ideas and guidance for guided reading sessions. The range of titles in the Reading Programme provides wide scope for further reading at every level.

The Usborne Reading Programme and the National Curriculum

The Usborne Reading Progamme is fully integrated with the National Curriculum for English at Key Stages 1 and 2, encouraging children to develop fluent and accurate reading across a range of texts, subjects and styles.

Selected titles from all levels of the Reading Programme are available as Guided Reading packs, comprising six copies of the book plus comprehensive teacher's notes. Guided Reading packs represent a selection of text types, and are carefully graded within levels 1-4 of the National Curriculum.

Text type: European folktale
NC level: 1C

Text type: Asian folktale
NC level: 1B

Text type: adapted children's classic
NC level: 1A

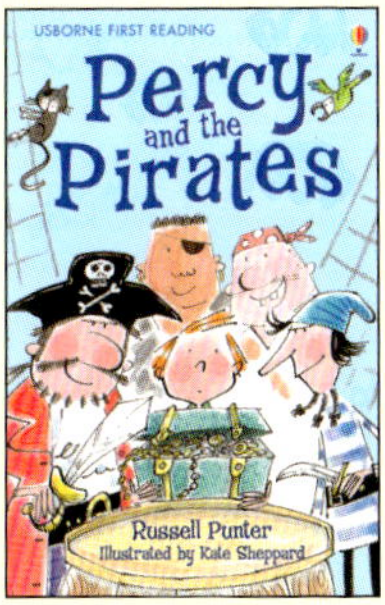

Text type:
original fiction
NC level: 2C

Text type:
original fiction
NC level: 2B

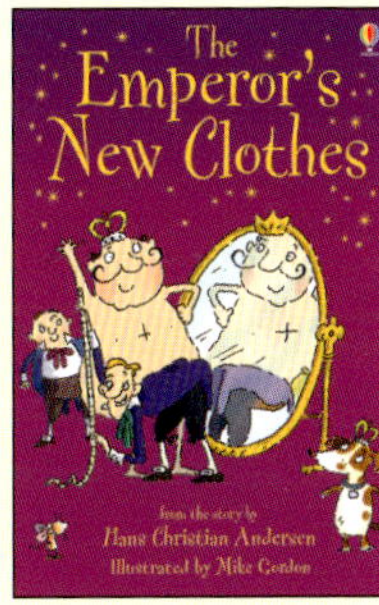

Text type:
classic fairytale
NC level: 2A

Text type:
myths and legends
NC level: 3C

Text type: adapted children's classic
NC level: 3B

Text type:
adapted classic
NC level: 3A

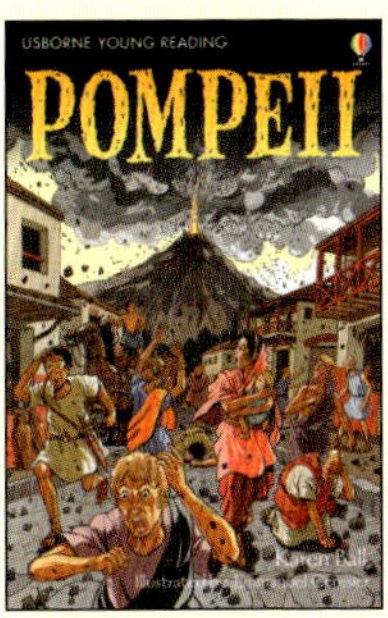

Text type:
non-fiction (history)
NC level: 4C

Text type:
biography
NC level: 4B

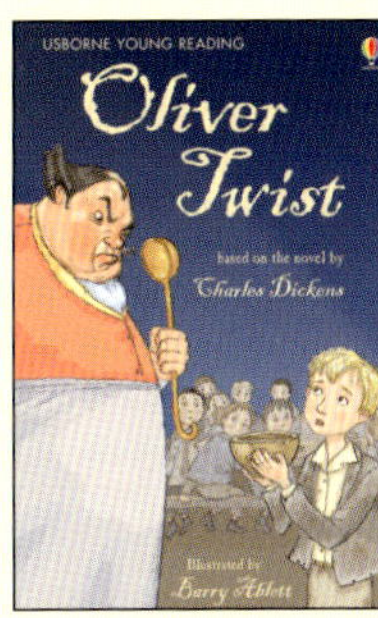

Text type:
adapted classic
NC level: 4A

The Usborne Reading

	Number of words	Themes
First Reading Level One National Curriculum level 1	up to 150	Classic tales (e.g. Aesop's Fables) and folktales
First Reading Level Two National Curriculum level 1	up to 250	As Level One, including less familiar folktales
First Reading Level Three National Curriculum level 1-2	up to 450	As Level Two plus original fiction and non-fiction (natural history life cycles)
First Reading Level Four National Curriculum level 2	up to 750	As Level Three plus classic fairy tales
Young Reading Series One National Curriculum level 2-3	1,000-1,500	Fairy tales, fantasy, fiction, non-fiction ("the story of...")
Young Reading Series Two National Curriculum level 3	2,000-2,500	As Series One plus adapted classics
Young Reading Series Three National Curriculum level 3-4	4,000-5,000	History, biographies classics

The elements above are intended as guidelines only, ar
whilst distinctions between different levels remain clea

Programme framework

Content	Vocabulary
Short single narrative followed by reading and comprehension puzzles	Simple everyday vocabulary, familiar items
Single narrative plus character sheets and/or maps, and puzzles	More descriptive and evocative vocabulary, always clear in context
Single narrative with repeated elements, plus character sheets and/or maps, no puzzles	Powerful verbs and adjectives, clear in context
Single narrative	More exotic elements and controlled use of idiom
Several linked stories or one longer narrative in chapters. Direct and indirect speech, intertextual references	Wide-ranging everyday vocabulary
Single narrative in chapters. Introduce irony and subplot, allow opportunity for inference and deduction	More challenging, building on Series One; specialist or technical terms explained
Single narrative in chapters. Assumes some relevant background knowledge	Building on Series Two, may assume knowledge of specialist or technical terms

xceptions may sometimes be made to individual pecifications in the interests of narrative or style.

Notes

Edited by Mairi Mackinnon

Designed by Katarina Dragoslavic

First published in 2008 by Usborne Publishing Ltd.,
83-85 Saffron Hill, London EC1N 8RT, England. www.usborne.com